WITNESS TO GENOCIDE

THE CHILDREN OF RWANDA

DRAWINGS BY
CHILD SURVIVORS
OF THE
RWANDAN GENOCIDE
OF 1994

EDITED BY
RICHARD A. SALEM

FOREWORD BY
HILLARY RODHAM CLINTON

"WITNESS TO GENOCIDE"

THE CHILDREN OF RWANDA

DRAWINGS BY
CHILD SURVIVORS
OF THE
RWANDAN GENOCIDE
OF 1994

Edited by
RICHARD A. SALEM

Foreword by
HILLARY RODHAM CLINTON

FRIENDSHIP PRESS • NEW YORK
NATIONAL COUNCIL OF THE CHURCHES
OF CHRIST IN THE USA

TO GRETA

Photos by Donna Ayerst   Design by Matthias Minde

Copyright ©2000 by Friendship Press, National Council of the Churches of Christ in the USA (NCC).

Published by Friendship Press with support from the NCC's Church World Service, Conflict Management Initiatives, and the W.K. Kellogg Foundation.

Editorial Offices: 475 Riverside Drive, New York, NY 10115

Distribution Offices: P.O. Box 37844, Cincinnati, OH 45222-0844

LIBRARY OF CONGRESS CATALOG-IN-PUBLICATION DATA

Witness to genocide: the children of Rwanda: drawings by child survivors of the Rwandan
genocide of 1994 / edited by Richard A. Salem : foreword by Hillary Rodham Clinton.
    p. cm.
  ISBN 0-377-00330-1
    1. Genocide — Rwanda — History — 20th century — Pictorial works. 2. Children and
genocide — Rwanda — History — 20th century — Pictorial works. 3. Children's
drawings — Rwanda. 4. Genocide in art. 5. Rwanda — Ethnic relations — History — 20th
century — Pictorial works. 6. Tutsi (African people) — Crimes
against — Rwanda — History — 20th century — Pictorial works. 7. Hutu (African
people) — Rwanda — politics and government — Pictorial works. I. Salem, Richard A.
DT450.435 .W58 2000
967.57104 — dc21   99-056238

CONTENTS

A MORAL NECESSITY

*Expanding the
Circle of Human Dignity*

FOREWORD BY

HILLARY RODHAM CLINTON

It is still impossible to believe that in the space of three months, 1 million people died in the Rwanda genocide of 1994. Nowhere in history have so many people been killed in such a short period of time. And yet, history teaches us that no one nation has a monopoly on evil. A 1996 UN report reminds us how war increasingly affects millions of innocent children all over the world. In the past decade alone, 2 million children have been killed in armed conflict; more than twice as many have been physically disabled; 12 million have been left homeless; and some 10 million have been psychologically traumatized, many from having been forced to witness or take part in acts of horrifying violence. In my travels from Uganda to Sri Lanka, I have time and time again seen firsthand the effects of such violence on children.

Violence does not just affect the soul of a child, it affects all aspects of development — psychological, physical, and cognitive growth are profoundly impacted. Imagine the thoughts of children who have witnessed the killing of a parent or were forced to become a soldier in a war they did not understand. Some children react to such circumstances with aggression and rage; others live in constant fear. More than 60 percent of the children interviewed in the aftermath of the Rwandan genocide said they did not care if they grew up. Providing for these children's recovery is not only the moral thing to do, it is absolutely necessary.

When I first looked at the drawings in this book, I immediately thought of the survivors I met in Uganda and Rwanda — their stories of loss and suffering and their plans for rebuilding their lives and communities. The resilience of their spirits stayed with me, and when I took a second look at *Witness to Genocide,* I realized that these drawings are not just depictions of brutal violence but are acts of recovery, healing, and hope. The very acts of talking, writing, and drawing are helping these children confront their past experiences and express their feelings about them. These children are finally beginning to understand what is happening inside of them so that healing may begin.

I remember Rwandan women survivors telling me that their first collective act in rebuilding their country would be to build a playground so all Rwandan children could come together to play and know that tomorrow would be better. These women understood that no nation can move ahead when its children are left behind. It is unconscionable that we still have not seen the circle of human dignity expanded to include all the children of our world. The collection before you not only demonstrates that point but is meant to inspire you to positive and forceful change. Ensuring that all the children of the world grow up in peace is an important, unfinished matter of business of the twentieth century and one of the great challenges of the next millennium. It is up to all adults to take on this challenge.

WHY TELL THE CHILDREN'S STORY NOW?

PREFACE BY

RICHARD A. SALEM

The loss of tens of thousands of children was not a byproduct of the genocide that gripped Rwanda for 100 days in 1994. It was an integral part of the Hutu government's plan to exterminate the Tutsi population. Other books have described in painful detail how this holocaust claimed 800,000 lives and created 300,000 orphans, while the rest of world looked the other way. *Witness to Genocide: The Children of Rwanda* tells the story through the eyes of the child survivors. Their drawings may be unsettling, but they are the images emblazoned on the minds of innocent children who witnessed the brutal slayings of their parents, siblings, and neighbors. For the children, these are the images that wake them in the middle of the night. Night after night. For the rest of us, these drawings are a reminder of what inevitably happens when the international community permits power-crazed leaders to foment genocidal violence. It is important that adults everywhere pay attention to the children's stories, as horrifying as they may be. In the words of Dr. Richard Sezibera, Rwandan ambassador to the United States:

> The tale of what happened during those dark days in Rwanda must be told again and again and again, not out of a morbid desire for gruesome tales, but out of a concern that the innocent dead should continuously sear the memories of the living. Only then can "never again" cease to be an empty cry.... It is important that we remember, for not only does collective memory contribute to the healing that comes

with shared pain, but it also gives hope that the world will remember and avoid the pitfalls of yesteryear.

This book is an outgrowth of a conflict management workshop I conducted for community leaders in Kigali, Rwanda, in 1997. At a follow-up meeting with a participant at the National Trauma Center, I saw some drawings by traumatized children who had been unable to talk about their experiences but who could draw the pictures that kept them awake at night. It was a short step from there to the decision to produce *Witness to Genocide: The Children of Rwanda*. The director of Friendship Press, a subsidiary of the National Council of the Churches of Christ in the USA (NCC), saw the drawings and expressed an immediate interest in publishing them. The Church World Service arm of the NCC supported the project with a grant assuring that a sub-

stantial royalty from the sale of each book will go directly to the severely underfunded counseling services available to Rwandan children. The W.K. Kellogg Foundation generously supported the publication and dissemination of the book. Additional funding came from Conflict Management Initiatives and employees of the U.S. Embassy in Kigali, who contributed through their 1999 St. Patrick's Day Walk/Run for Charity.

Drawings in this book were spontaneously created by child survivors during trauma counseling some three to four years after the genocide ended. The captions are their own. The photographs were taken at a school and at an orphanage where trauma advisers work with the staff and children. The names used with the photographs are fictitious, but the stories are true.

Witness to Genocide: The Children of Rwanda reflects the work and support of many individuals. Josee Nytere, a trauma counselor, painstakingly compiled and translated the captions on the drawings. The chapter "The Children" is based largely on interviews with her, with former National Trauma Center President Evode Kazasomako, and with Dr. Munyandamutsa Nasson, who also made available his unpublished paper, "Ces Enfants de Nulle Part: à la Rechercher de Sens et de Reperes," (Rwanda: Children from Nowhere in Search of Feelings and Landmarks). Important contributions to this chapter were also made by Dr. Magne Raundalen, director of research for children at the Center for Crisis Psychology in Bergen, Norway. He made available an interview published in UNICEF's *First*

Call for Children (April 1994) and two unpublished papers, "How War Affects Children — What Can We Do?" which was presented at Huber University, Wuhan, China, in 1998, and "Hjelp Til Barn Etter Kirg — Barndommen varer hele livet" (Help for Children after War — Childhood Lasts for Life).

This book is not intended to provide a full description of the complex events that led to or occurred during the genocide. Three important books documenting the genocide that were sources for this book are *We Wish to Inform You That Tomorrow We Will Be Killed with Our Families: Stories from Rwanda,* by Philip Gourevitch (Farrar Straus and Giroux, 1998); *The Rwanda Crisis: History of a Genocide,* by Gerrard Prunier (Columbia University Press, 1995); and *Rwanda: Death, Despair, and Defiance,* by Rakiya Omaar and Alex de Waal (African Rights, London, 1994). Additional information was gleaned from the web site of the Embassy of the Republic of Rwanda in Washington, D.C., www.rwandemb.org, and from the report *Child-Headed Households in Rwanda,* prepared for UNICEF by World Vision.

Ambassador Sezibera was asked to contribute to this book after I heard about the success of the Children's Parliament he convened in December 1998 when he was president of the Committee on Social Affairs in the Rwandan Parliament. In addition to writing a chapter, he has been a valuable source of information and support. The invitation to First Lady Hillary Rodham Clinton to write the foreword was based on her deep concern and compassion for children everywhere as expressed in her actions and words. Others who made important contributions are Alice LeMaistre, public affairs officer for the U. S. Information Service (USIS), who introduced me to Rwanda and encouraged this project from the outset; Roger Burgess, who was director of Friendship Press when this project was launched; human-rights attorney Jane Rocamora for her guidance in Kigali and the United States; Sanna Longden and Erica Salem, for editing the manuscript; art therapist Marian Liebmann for her support throughout this project; Randy Naylor, NCC director of communications; Donna Burgess, former executive assistant to the NCC general secretary; Eugenie Kanzayire, USIS program officer in Kigali; Winifred Farbman, Al Farbman, David Forte, Judith Hines, Zoe Salem, and Susanne Salem Schatz for their comments on the manuscript and design; Eileen Cooper of the Academy of Legal and Technical Translation; Paula Tachau and Prudentienne Seward for their assistance with translations; Joe Maizlish, who introduced me to the work of Dr. Magne Raundalen; David Hess; the Rev. Edward White; Debra Amos; and Jennifer Berman, both for her support of the project and for recommending the very talented Matt Minde to do the design.

Royalties from the sale of each book and all proceeds after costs will be used to support the treatment of traumatized survivors of the genocide in Rwanda. Additional copies of the book may be ordered directly from Friendship Press Distribution Office, P.O. Box 37844, Cincinnati, OH 45222 (1-800-889-5733) or Conflict Management Initiatives (CMI), 1225 Oak Avenue, Evanston IL 60202 (www.cmi-salem.org). Contributions for the treatment of traumatized children in Rwanda can be sent to CMI at the same address. CMI is a tax-exempt organization under Section 501 (c) (3) of the Internal Revenue Code.

ABOUT THE CONTRIBUTORS

RICHARD A. SALEM,
a mediator and trainer, is president of Conflict Management Initiatives, a not-for-profit organization that supports and encourages the use of mediation and other collaborative processes to manage community conflicts.

HILLARY RODHAM CLINTON
is the First Lady of the United States of America. Her work has taken her to Rwanda and neighboring countries of East Africa.

RICHARD SEZIBERA, M.D.,
is ambassador from the Republic of Rwanda to the United States. He served as a doctor in the Rwandese Patriotic Army with the rank of major and chaired the Commission on Social Issues in the Parliament of Rwanda. He convened Rwanda's first Children's Parliament in 1998.

GRETA SALEM, PH.D.,
is a professor of political science at Alverno College in Milwaukee.

DONNA AYERST
is a freelance photographer based in Mozambique. She formerly lived and worked in Rwanda.

MATTHIAS MINDE
is a freelance graphic designer based in Chicago.

1.
THE GENOCIDE

800,000 Lives

in 100 Days

RICHARD A. SALEM AND

GRETA SALEM

On the night of April 6, 1994, General Juvenal Habyarimana, the Hutu president of Rwanda, was killed when a ground-based missile mysteriously shot down his plane as it prepared to land at the nation's capital city of Kigali. Within the hour, a group of Hutu extremists who were at the heart of the president's powerful and corrupt inner circle formally launched a systematic campaign of genocide designed to remove every Tutsi and some moderate Hutus from the face of Rwanda. The effort fell short, lasting barely three months. But in that time some 800,000 Rwandans were slaughtered. A nation and its children, including hundreds of thousands of orphans who had witnessed the brutal killings of their families, friends, and neighbors, were left reeling in trauma.

The genocide did not come as a total surprise to everyone. Three months earlier, a government informant had provided detailed plans of the genocide to Major

General Romeo Dallaire, commander of the United Nations peacekeeping force in Rwanda. General Dallaire had transmitted this information to his superiors at the United Nations in New York and requested permission to take preventive action. He was instructed, however, to take no action beyond sharing the information with the United States, French, and Belgian embassies in Kigali and with the president of Rwanda. The international community neither acknowledged that genocide had been planned nor intervened when it took place.

Many words have been written about the remarkable circumstances surrounding the genocide of the Tutsi, but perhaps none present as cogent a summary as the apology uttered by a contrite President Bill Clinton on March 25, 1998, when he traveled to Kigali to pay his nation's respects to the victims.

During the 90 days that began on April 6 in 1994, Rwanda experienced the most intensive slaughter in this blood-filled century.... Families murdered in their homes, people hunted down as they fled ... through farmland and woods as if they were animals. ...People gathered seeking refuge in churches by the thousand, in hospitals, in schools. And when they were found, the old and sick, women and children alike, they were killed — killed because their identity card said they were Tutsi or because they had a Tutsi parent, or because someone thought they looked like a Tutsi, or slain like thousands of Hutus because they protected Tutsis or would not countenance a policy that sought to wipe out people who just the day before, and for years before, had been their friends and neighbors . . . .

It is important that the world know that these killings were not spontaneous or accidental. . . . Not the result of ancient tribal struggles. . . . These events grew from a policy aimed at the systematic destruction of a people. The ground for violence was carefully prepared, the airwaves poisoned with hate, casting the Tutsi as scapegoats for the problems of Rwanda, denying their humanity. All of this was done clearly to make it easy for otherwise reluctant people to participate in wholesale slaughter. Lists of victims, name by name, were actually drawn up in advance.

The international community . . . must bear its share of responsibility for this tragedy as well. We did not act quickly enough after the killing began. We should not have allowed the refugee camps to become a safe haven for the killers. We did not immediately call these crimes by their name: genocide.

In 1999 an independent panel was commissioned by the UN secretary-general to investigate the international community's failure either to take steps to prevent the genocide or to respond when it broke out. The panel placed the blame directly on UN officials and member nations — especially the United States — that put pressure on the UN to curtail its response.

THE PEOPLE OF RWANDA

The Hutus and Tutsis, who comprise 99 percent of the population of Rwanda, had not always been violent antagonists. They had lived together with the Twa — the original inhabitants of Rwanda and the remaining 1 percent of the population — for centuries in their kingdom known as "the land of a thousand hills." Their ethnic origins are not clear, but many believe that the Tutsis, typically taller than Hutus and with other distinct physical characteristics, entered the region from the north. The differences have been blurred by time. All Rwandans are called Banyarwanda, speak the same language, share a culture, live on the same hills, and for centuries

"Why am I being killed?"

have intermarried. The Tutsis were traditionally cattle owners; Hutus worked the land. Tutsis comprised only an estimated 9 to 15 percent of the population, but as owners of valuable cattle they enjoyed a higher status than Hutu farmers and achieved a disproportionate share of political power.

During the colonial period, the differences between Hutus and Tutsis assumed new importance. European settlers were attracted to the Tutsis, who were physically more appealing to the outsiders. It suited the Belgians, who controlled the country after World War I, to create a hierarchy beneath them with the Tutsis at the top, thus giving credence to the myth of Tutsi racial superiority. All Rwandans were required to carry identification cards designating their heritage. The fact that it was impossible to determine ethnicity solely by physical appearance did not deter the Belgians. They simply designated families owning ten or more cows as Tutsi. By limiting Hutu access to education, the colonial rulers further solidified the position of the Tutsi elite at the expense of the Hutu population.

Tutsi leaders, like many others in Africa, sought independence for their country after World War II. Fearful of losing control, Belgium responded to these demands by supporting a violent coup waged by a Hutu opposition group. Thus in 1957 Tutsi domination came to an end. The pent-up anger of aggrieved Hutus, encouraged by the country's new Hutu leadership, led to mob violence and tens of thousands of Tutsi deaths. Hundreds of thousands fled across the borders into Uganda,

Burundi, and Tanzania. The violence, the purging of Tutsis from positions of power, and the exodus across borders continued after Rwanda gained its independence in 1962 and sporadically for another ten years until a division between Hutu factions led to a second coup, which brought General Habyarimana to power.

THE HUTUS IN POWER

The new president publicly pledged an end to ethnic politics but proceeded to establish a single, totalitarian party, the Mouvement Revolutionnaire National pour le Developpement (MRND). The violence subsided for several years, but there was no end to the discrimination against the Tutsi population.

Requiring all citizens — even children — to become members of the MRND made it possible for the government to keep track of every designated Tutsi. The MRND was structured throughout the country with layers that began in the 12 prefectures, moved down through 147 communes, then into thousands of sectors, and, finally, into cells of 100 households. Local officials were selected by the MRND's leadership. State permission was required by anyone wanting to change residence.

Through many of his twenty-two years in office, President Habyarimana was under pressure to bring about reforms. A deteriorating economy led to protests throughout the country and exacerbated long-standing tensions between Hutus from the south of Rwanda and

A firefight between the government forces and the Rwandese Patriotic Army

those from the north. Externally, Western donors demanded political and economic reform and supported the demands of Rwanda's neighbors that the estimated 1 million Tutsi refugees who had been displaced from their homeland be repatriated.

There was a serious military threat as well. Tutsi exiles, who had received valuable training and experience when they served in the armed forces that brought President Yoweri Musevani to power in Uganda, began making guerrilla incursions into Rwanda in the late 1980s. The exiles established the Rwandese Patriotic Front (RPF) in Uganda in 1987 to bring about the repatriation of Tutsi refugees to Rwanda. In 1990, after the RPF could make no headway in its efforts to negotiate with the Habyarimana regime, its military arm, the Rwandese Patriotic Army (RPA), launched a civil war. This formidable army might well have toppled the Habyarimana regime had it not been for the military and logistical support provided to the Rwandan government by France; an RPF victory, the French government feared, would seriously diminish its influence in Rwanda.

A POLICY OF GENOCIDE

Although the pressures on President Habyarimana forced him to an international negotiating table with the RPF in Arusha, Tanzania, in June 1992, he was continually accused of failing to negotiate in good faith. It took fourteen months to reach an agreement that called for (1) a transitional Rwandan government with repre-sentation of all political forces in the country and the RPF, (2) a UN peacekeeping force to assure a non-violent transition, (3) a broadly representative national army, and (4) the repatriation of refugees. The RPF had already agreed to a cease-fire and would now await a peace accord that would never be implemented.

President Habyarimana gave lip service to the Arusha Peace Accord, but extremists in his inner circle denounced it and used every tactic at their command to prevent its implementation while continuing to lay the foundation for genocide. For nearly a year they had been using the radio and other media blatantly to incite the Hutu populace to turn on their Tutsi neighbors. Asserting that the RPF was planning to confiscate land owned by Hutu farmers, the Hutu extremists urged them to strike a preemptive blow by killing Tutsis and taking their land.

The formation of a UN peacekeeping force in Rwanda was hampered by the agency's earlier failed effort to end internal violence in Somalia. Many countries refused to commit troops to another African foray, and those that did ordered their contingents not to risk their own safety. So they did not intervene to stop the mounting violence or the distribution of arms to civilians, and their response was minimal when genocide began.

President Habyarimana was returning home on April 6, 1994, from a meeting in Tanzania, where the presidents of Rwanda's neighboring countries had admonished him for delaying implementation of the peace accord. It is not known what was on his mind as his plane prepared to land in Kigali, but at least some members of his inner circle were fearful he could not withstand the pressure for change. They responded with uncanny speed and precision when his plane was shot down. They immediately set up roadblocks while armed troops and local political leaders, carrying lists of already targeted individuals, began rounding up and executing the regime's political enemies. The following day Rwanda's prime minister and ten soldiers from Belgium's UN contingent assigned to protect her were assassinated.

Genocide had started. It soon spread to every city and rural area in Rwanda, onto the hills where Hutus and Tutsis lived side by side. The perpetrators utilized the army, militia, and police as well as the tightly controlled network of local political leaders and officials who reached into virtually every home in the country. No Tutsi was to be spared, Hutus were instructed. Hutu

"Where shall we flee to now?"

farmers and others were called upon to kill their Tutsi neighbors and share in the spoils. Those who refused — and thousands of Hutus did — were at risk of becoming victims themselves. These orders came through channels from the highest ranks of government, were repeated at local meetings, and resounded across the countryside over the extremist-controlled radio station. As the directors of the human-rights group African Rights later observed, the extremists were not on the fringes of Rwandan society but in the heart of the government and therefore had all the power of government at their disposal. The instruments of death were guns and grenades, for those who had them. Most victims were killed with machetes, knives, and *masus* — wooden clubs spiked with nails. Some of the victims were burned to death hiding above the ceilings of their homes. Others were thrown into pit latrines. It was important to kill the women because they would bear the next generation of Tutsis, and the children because they were the future soldiers of the RPF.

Three months after it began, the holocaust came to an end as the army of the RPF swept across Rwanda, killing thousands of Hutus who were in its path, and driving more than 100,000 Hutu military and other armed opponents as well as other Rwandan Hutus across the border into Zaire. There, in an ironic change of fortune, they were housed and nourished in UN refugee camps, which soon became bases for Hutu guerrilla attacks on Rwanda.

Many Tutsi children escaped violent death but witnessed it from hiding places behind houses, in trees, in the bush, or beneath the bodies of the dead. An estimated 70 percent of them watched as their families, friends, or neighbors were brutally shot, stabbed, clubbed, or hacked to death. More than 90 percent experienced a death in the family. Hundreds of thousands of children were orphaned, creating new classifications for Rwanda's youngest generation: "unaccompanied children" and "child-headed households."

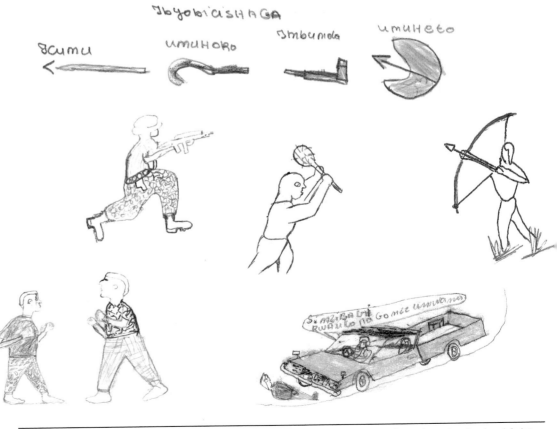

Instruments of genocide: spear, machete, guns, bow and arrow, grenades, "masu", hit-and-run, hand-to-hand fighting

SINAVUKIYEINTAMBARA MU

MÈRE DE MOI

"My mother"

"Soldiers killing neighbors"

HOW THE WAR STARTED

This illustration shows the beginning of the massacres in cartoon form. The text is translated below, keyed to the corresponding letters in the picture.

A

"The President is dead. You can kill everyone! Don't even spare the fetuses."

B

"I have them surrounded; they won't escape."

C

"Please forgive us!"

D

"When the militia was killing my people" "Kill him quickly!"

E

"I have 25 francs (from a slain Tutsi). When would I have gotten that much money if I stayed at home?!"

F

"They are going to kill us, we are finished!" "Mama!" "Oh, Jesus!"

G

"I have finished them! They can't escape!"

H

"I have been saved, but my entire family has been killed. I have become an orphan; where shall I live?"

I

"Do you have a family, child?" "No, they all have been killed!"

"How the war started in Rwanda"

Aba bagabo bali batemye bagenzi babo

"Men killing friends"

"I am stabbing you with my sword."

"What happened to the Tutsis in 1994"

"Genocide"

"The genocide"

"She doesn't know what is happening.
He asks, 'Are you a Tutsi?'
She begins to feel afraid."

"A man is shot even though his hands are raised."

A "Oh, they are killing me!"
B "Oh, Papa!"
C "My father did nothing but he is
   being killed!"
D "I shot him!"
E "If you miss, I'll hit him with my masu!"
F "I am afraid!" "Let's go faster!"

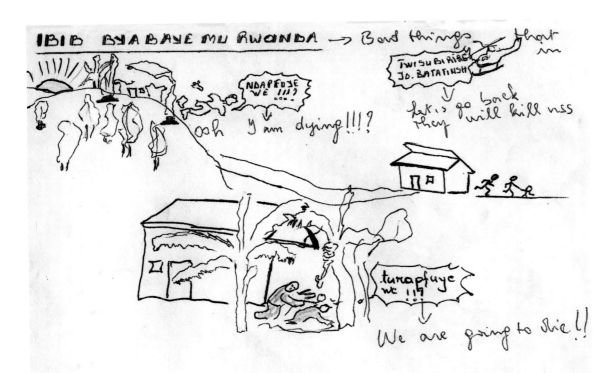

"Bad things that happened in Rwanda"

"Have mercy my child!"
"There is no mercy. Our objective is
to finish you off!"

"My cousin saw them and climbed a tree... they finally caught my mother's sister and killed her; I don't know exactly where."

"Death was everywhere, even in front of the church."

"A militiaman carrying bloodstained knife"

CANDIDE, 14

"You can kill me, but God will ask you why," Candide recalls her friend saying just before she was slain by a militiaman. Candide was nine years old at the time. From her hiding place in the woods, she also saw a man enter a house and kill two people. When the woods were set ablaze, she and others fled deeper into the bush.

"The world looked on in impotent horror as carnage was wreaked on their young minds and bodies. It should not look on as they struggle through the process of healing."

— AMBASSADOR RICHARD SEZIBERA

2.
THE
CHILDREN

A Nation Struggles to Heal Its

Betrayed Youth and Reclaim Its Future

RICHARD A. SALEM AND

GRETA SALEM

Evode Kazasomako remembers rounding up child survivors when the war was over. He was a social worker in one of the displacement camps established for the homeless. "There were children everywhere," he recalled. "They had been hiding in forests and swamps. Some had had only grass to eat. Many had untreated wounds. They needed help, but even when it was safe, they were afraid to come out of the bush. They had lost everything and trusted no one. We had to go in and coax them out."

Tens of thousands of children were cared for in the camps, but as many as 300,000 others returned to their parentless homes or villages after the genocide and became members of an estimated 85,000 "child-headed households." There they fended off adults who tried to exploit them and fought for survival in conditions of dire poverty. They had virtually no opportunities for work, schooling or health care. Many of those youngsters were eventually reunited with their families, adopted or reached adulthood, but an estimated 60,000 such households remained as recently as 1998.

Kazasomako and his colleagues faced many problems trying to care for the children who came into the camps. "Some were very aggressive," he recalled. "Some were numbed and could not speak. Others just cried. Many were unable to sleep at night. Bed wetting was common. Some would get sick from overeating; others could hardly eat at all. We soon learned that virtually everyone had 'flashbacks,' haunting pictures of the genocide. We had never seen anything like this."

THE CAUSES AND SYMPTOMS OF TRAUMA

When the war ended, Kazasomako knew nothing about trauma. "There was no such word in the Kinyarwandan language," he said. "Nor were there any psychiatrists or child psychologists or therapists in Rwanda then. At first we thought the children's wartime living conditions had caused these disorders and that if we fed, clothed, and played with them, the problems would disappear. The symptoms did abate for some, but they persisted or recurred in many children. It was only after UNICEF [United Nations International Children's Education Fund] and the international NGOs [nongovernmental organiza-

"We have lost our parents. Can you help us?" "You look traumatized."

tions] began working with us that we learned about trauma. Then, when parents and teachers told us they were observing the same behaviors that we had seen in the displacement camps, we understood the immensity of the problem. It was everywhere."

The challenge to the caretakers was compounded by parents who did not want the children to talk about the genocide. "There were cultural taboos against discussing mental illness," Kazasomako noted. "We realized that many of the parents were traumatized, too. They were unable to understand their own behaviors. They were in a state of denial."

Dr. Munyandamutsa Naason, a Rwandan psychiatrist who returned home from abroad to work with the traumatized children, found many of them living in a cultural vacuum. "In Rwandan society," he explained, "the identity or persona of a child is deeply rooted in his or her relationships with parents, siblings, and community. These relationships have a spiritual quality and the child is taught never to forget where she comes from or to whom he belongs. All of this was obliterated for the survivors when trusted members of the community turned on Tutsi families. The children lost their frame of reference. What could they believe? Whom could they trust?

"Some children have developed neuroses, others have epileptic fits. Psychosomatic illnesses are common. They cannot concentrate in the classroom. We try to get these youngsters to play and behave like

children, but they tell us they cannot be children because they have no parents and they must care for their younger brothers and sisters. Yet they lack the wherewithal to be 'parents.'"

Dr. Magne Raundalen, director of research for children at the Center for Crisis Psychology in Bergen, Norway, has studied the impact of violence on children in war zones in fourteen countries. He describes trauma as a

response to a life-threatening event that overwhelms a person and renders him or her helpless. The experience "leads to changes in the sensory system, and will be stored in a person's memory as anxiety and

tension," he says. "Children are tormented by traumatic sense impressions. . . . Images and sound are constantly bothering the child by returning . . . as vivid, sudden, and uncontrolled recollections."

Dr. Raundalen presents a disheartening view of the world as seen through the eyes of a child who has survived a war. A child can feel betrayed, he says, when the traditional family and community networks that are relied upon for protection and comfort during times of crisis are fragmented or destroyed, when the adult world — the world order that the child trusted — has collapsed.

"Probably the most destructive experience for a child is the knowledge that his parents can no longer provide protection in times of war. . . . Children in war express the feeling that the entire adult society has derailed and thus collapsed. . . . They are not able to obtain peace of mind. . . . The only comfort many of the children find in this context is through a deep intense hatred of the officially declared enemy."

HEALING TRAUMA

Healing trauma requires more than food, security, and a return to normal life, according to Dr. Raundalen. Effective treatment requires "open and trusting communication" about the precipitating events. Yet, these experiences, he says, can be so "disturbing, painful, tormenting, and overwhelming," that the child may

"Don't think about the death of your parents. Come, play football."

not talk about them unless "encouraged or sometimes even pushed" to do so. Instead, the child "suppresses the bad memories and the feelings associated with them." Methods of healing trauma, he notes, use children's natural ways of expressing themselves: drawing, writing, singing, dancing, and praying. Such methods must, however, be applied systematically by trained persons who can assure proper follow-up.

The Rwandan government's social ministries established the National Trauma Center in 1995. Evode Kazasomako was the first director. UNICEF funded the effort and assigned two psychologists from Belgium to provide training. Other NGOs also provided trauma treatment services. Within two years, some 20,000 teachers, ministers, orphanage staff, and other caregivers had been trained to recognize trauma and employ some basic methods for its alleviation. The need for counselors, however, far outweighed the help that was available. In an effort to provide additional support for trauma treatment, in 1999 the Rwandan government moved the National Trauma Center into the Ministry of Health. The ministry is committed to expanding treatment programs into the prefectures outside of Kigali, but the money available for this work is extremely limited.

EUGENIE'S STORY

"Time itself will not heal trauma," Dr. Raundalen warns. The story of Eugenie, who was taken to the trauma center in 1999, illustrates how the symptoms can be dormant for a time but will ultimately emerge. Eugenie, age seventeen, was living with an aunt and attending a boarding school outside of Kigali. Her teachers knew that she had lost her family, but they were unaware of what she had experienced as a twelve-year-old during the genocide. The children at school would sometimes talk about the war when they were alone. It was on one such evening that

Eugenie declared that she had lost most of her family in the genocide. A classmate taunted her, "If your family died, why are you still alive?" Eugenie did not respond. She slipped away from the group and went to bed. When she awoke in the morning, she was unable to speak.

School officials called her aunt, who took her to the hospital and then to the trauma center's clinic. Eugenie tried to communicate with her counselor; she moved her lips, but the words would not come out. When the counselor gave her a pen and paper, Eugenie wrote about witnessing her mother's death while hiding behind a tree. She had seen her mother hacked with a machete and recalled the blood streaming from her neck. Eugenie had been petrified. She remembered closing her eyes and wishing that she could die. She ran into the bush and survived there until she was rescued by soldiers.

Eugenie returned to the clinic five times. At each session she would write her story and express the guilt she felt as a survivor. This was the first time she had shared her experiences with anybody. Her voice finally returned to normal and she went back to school. Trauma counseling had enabled her to confront her past so that she could survive the present and the future.

Hutu children were also traumatized by the war; some by the violence they witnessed, others because they followed instructions and became violent themselves, wielding machetes or improvised weapons during the holocaust. After the war, many Hutu children lived as orphans in the violence-ridden refugee camps in Zaire and Tanzania, which were controlled by the leaders of the genocide. Some lost or became separated from their parents during the flight from Rwanda or on the trip home when they were repatriated.

"Whenever I wake up in the middle of the night, I remember the many bad things I saw."

TRAUMA TREATMENT AS PEACE EDUCATION

Failure to treat trauma can be devastating for both the children and the society. Lack of treatment "can inhibit the intellectual, emotional, and behavioral development of a child," warns Dr. Raundalen. Severely traumatized children can be aggressive, Dr. Nasson adds, and a disturbing number tend to be violent when conflicts arise. "Many children in Rwanda lack adult role models to teach them empathy, tolerance, and love which are normally learned from parents," Dr. Naason says. "If we do not find a way to teach them, the aggression will continue."

Dr. Raundalen sees aggression and violence as a natural outgrowth of the children's experience of genocide. "Trauma victims are surrounded by the memories of the critical event," he notes. In responding to these anxiety-producing images, they may act in ways "that do not correspond to reality." Some children can be expected to demonstrate "inexplicable aggression toward the child himself or others." A traumatized child will have difficulty contributing to the building of a peaceful society with democratic institutions. "How can you start thinking about peace with the picture of dead bodies before your eyes ... when the picture of throats being cut comes before you every day?" he asks.

"Any peace education that talks about tolerance and negotiation without addressing the children's rage and anger...won't work." Trauma treatment, he emphasizes, is "peace education."

THE TIME OF THE WAR

"I am traumatized by the memories of the day they cut off my arm and leg."

"Whenever I play with other children, I try to forget the things I saw."

TRAUMA

This drawing, titled *"What Concerns Psychological Trauma,"* shows discussions about trauma between children and counselors and among each other.

Ⓐ

"Orphanage"

Ⓑ

"Let's dance so we don't become traumatized."

Ⓒ

"Let's dance together instead of being alone."

Ⓓ

"These children are playing ball so they can forget what happened to their families."

Ⓔ

"This child pretends to be alone."

Ⓕ

"This child is alone and remembers what happened during the war — he is traumatized."

Ⓖ

"This child is sick, he is in bed, dreaming that they are cutting him into pieces."

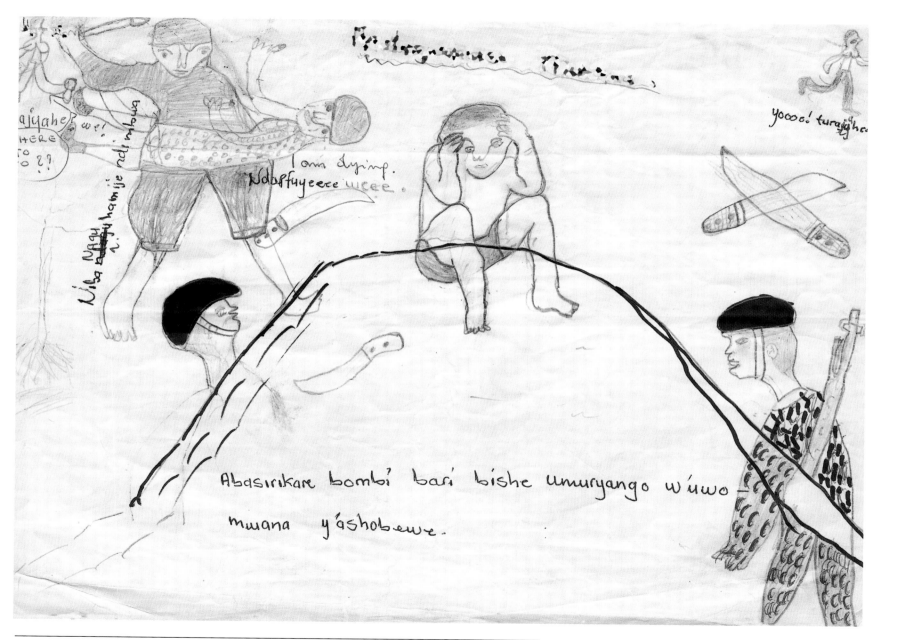

"He saw his parents being killed. He has no words to express his feelings."

THE REFUGEE ORPHAN

This drawing shows a child fleeing from the militias, hiding in a sorghum field and eventually being rescued by persons in a truck who are searching for unattended children.

(A)

"Come rescue me — they are killing me!"

(B)

"Catch him and I will cut him in two!"

(C)

"My machete is filled with blood; they are finished."

(D)

"The church is full of dead bodies."

(E)

"For God's sake, forgive us!"
"I am dying!"

(F)

"Get out of the bush!"

(G)

"Let's go to the orphanage. This car will take us to compassion which will be our substitute parents."

A woman laments, "It is not my fault that they were killed."

"Militiaman chasing refugees"

"Come quickly or I'll leave you here!"

36

"Genocide"

"Don't miss her! Shoot!"

Red Cross / Red Crescent camp

"Shall we ever have a child again?"
"Keep quiet! They might hear you and return!"

THE TIME OF THE WAR

"This child is becoming traumatized because he hears guns; they tell him not to worry."

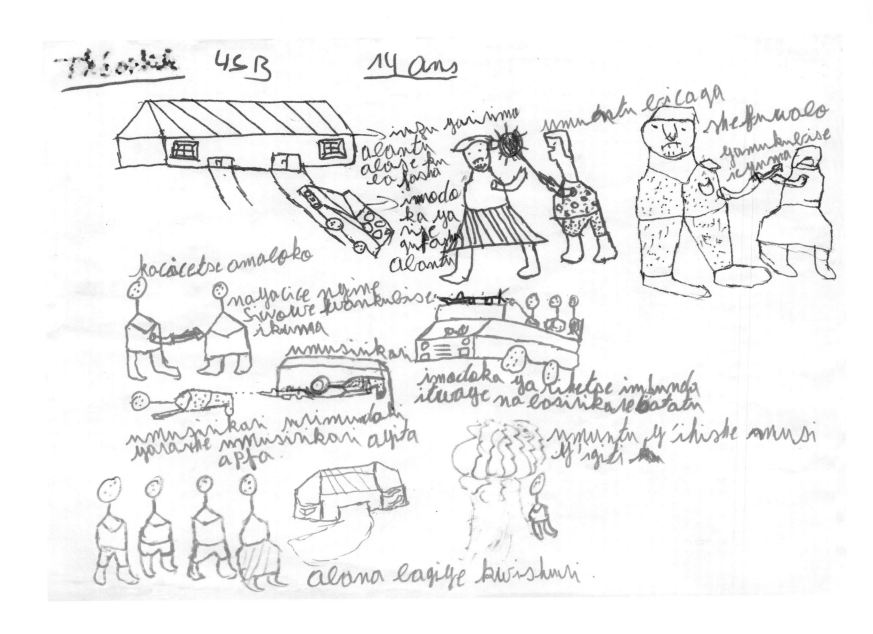

This drawing depicts some of the child's bad dreams: "I have no arms and it is your fault!"

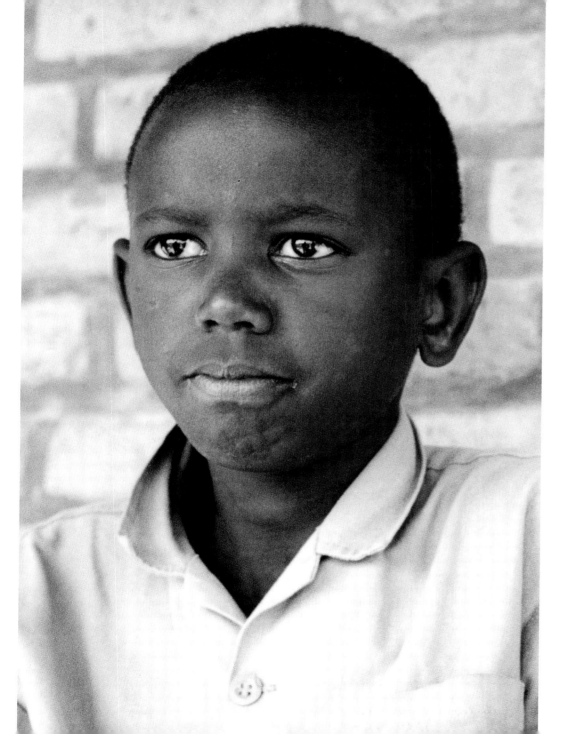

JEAN PIERRE, 9

Jean Pierre was four years old when he witnessed the deaths of his mother and brother. He was hiding under his house until it was set afire and he fled undetected. Five years later, Jean Pierre dreams of guns and machetes.

"Rwanda's children are part of our future. They need to remember what happened to them, but they must also be released from this trauma so they will be able to function as responsible adult leaders."

— AMBASSADOR RICHARD SEZIBERA

41

3.
THE FUTURE
OF RWANDA

Help the Children

Tell Their Story

RICHARD SEZIBERA, M.D.

Every war, every conflict, every horrendous event, if it becomes too horrible, numbs the mind and chokes the emotions. In retrospect, it can often be narrowed to one scene that the mind grasps, subconsciously churns over, and then indelibly imprints on itself as the defining event of the unimaginable horror. The drawings in *Witness to Genocide* bring this out in a powerful way. I am humbled to be part of this process that commits the horror of genocide to the collective memory of the world.

A DEFINING MOMENT

I was witness to such a defining scene at the peak of the genocide when the battalion with which I was serving as a field medical officer encountered one lit-

tle boy, playing in the sand amid the flying bullets. His mother had bathed and dressed him in his best clothes and placed him in the middle of the road, hoping against hope that the genocidal forces in the area would, at the very least, spare a child. But she knew that the radio had been exhorting the killers not to spare even the little Tutsi children, for they would then grow up and produce other Tutsis. So the desperate mother came out of hiding and led the killers away from her little boy by screaming and running in the opposite direction. We later found her mutilated body some distance from her child.

And so, we rescued this one little boy, still playing in the sand amid the flying bullets. The first question he asked me when I got to him was, "Why are the Tutsis so bad? Why was I born a Tutsi?"

When I think of the horror and poignancy of the genocide against the Tutsis in Rwanda in 1994, my mind comes back to that moment, again and again.

There were many orphaned children, many bodies of men, women, and children murdered for the crime of existence. But that moment for me signifies all the evil that was Rwanda in 1994. I notice that the same question the little boy asked me is expressed in a drawing in this book, with a victim begging for his life and promising never to be a Tutsi again.

The tale of what happened during those dark days in Rwanda must be told again and again and again, not

"I promise never to be Tutsi again!"

out of a morbid desire for gruesome tales but out of a concern that the innocent dead should continuously sear the memories of the living. Only then can "never again" cease to be an empty cry.

THE IMPORTANCE OF REMEMBERING

Memory is extremely important, collective memory more so. With the advent of the global village, we now have a tremendous capacity to do good in the world. The corollary, however, is that evil committed anywhere now affects each of us in a more powerful and visible way. It is important that we remember, for not only does collective memory contribute to the healing that comes with shared pain, but it also gives hope that the world will remember and avoid the pitfalls of yesteryear.

The children of Rwanda live with terrible memories. At an age when children elsewhere enjoy the protection of their parents and receive from them the all-important moral certitudes and impressions of the goodness and sanctity of human life, the children of Rwanda have seen their parents and loved ones killed by their neighbors. Instead of seeing the adults as bastions against the real and imagined terrors of childhood, they have been exposed to the baser side of humanity. They have had to deal with a magnitude of evil and cruelty from adults that their young and growing minds can hardly contain.

Tens of thousands of the children in need of assistance are members of child-headed households where boys and girls as young as thirteen must look after their younger siblings at a time when they can hardly look after themselves. Healing for these children will take a long time and will require resources that are unfortunately available in pitifully small amounts in comparison to the task.

RESTORING NORMALCY

The children of Rwanda were not only victims. Some also became killers at the behest of the government of the day. Instead of teaching the children to grow up as responsible citizens in a society respectful of human rights and protective of fundamental freedoms, the genocidal government made violence respectable to young people in their formative years and encouraged them to apply almost insurmountable peer pressure to those who would have rejected genocide and chosen the path of sanity. Stories are told in Rwanda of teachers devising disingenuous ways of teaching arithmetic to six- and seven-year-olds: "If there were seven Tutsis in a market and four were killed, how many would you have left?"

With their government promoting hatred and institutionalizing discrimination, the children of Rwanda did not learn how to live in a tolerant pluralistic society where they could experience peace and harmony with themselves and others. Rwanda must help all of its

children achieve such a society, both those whose families were killed in the genocide and the thousands of children who participated in the slaughter and became mass murderers in their own right.

One child who is a killer is traumatic to his society; thousands of children who are killers should be traumatic to humanity. Many countries have had intense periods of national soul searching every time their children have committed acts of violence. Their citizens have grappled with the very difficult issues of culpability after these events have taken place. Some countries have even lowered the age for legal culpability as a result of violent episodes by the young. Perhaps nowhere has the problem been as acute as in Rwanda.

How does one deal with the hundreds of thousands of children — some as young as nine — who either became killers or saw their families become shrines for the celebration of killing? What moral certitudes can these children have in life and how can they be shown that normal societies hold life sacrosanct? These are issues Rwanda is struggling to address. There are no easy answers, no facile solutions.

Rwanda's children are part of our future. They need to remember what happened to them, but they also must be released from their traumas so they will be able to function as responsible adults and leaders. They need help from sympathetic adults who can provide the children with the opportunities they need to externalize their memories and put the pain and anxiety to rest.

Only in this way can they be part of the march to a better future as the twenty-first century dawns. We adults must assist them in this endeavor.

THE CHILDREN'S PARLIAMENT

In December 1998, a cross-section of Rwandan children convened at a Children's Parliament in the legislative chambers in Kigali to discuss their past and debate the prospects for their future. The First Lady of the Land chaired the proceedings. Attendees included members of Parliament, government officials, and representatives of UNICEF and NGOs dealing with children's issues. For two days the children debated issues that concern them. They discussed children's rights and the importance that society should attach to them, and they debated the role that they as children should play in the building of a better society in Rwanda. They shared with the adult decision makers their vision of a discrimination-free society, one that would enable them to achieve their full potential. The young participants came from cities, villages, and remote rural areas. There were Tutsis and Hutus, children living in family settings and those from child-headed households. Some were in school; others, struggling just to survive, did not attend school.

It became evident during the Children's Parliament that even though Rwanda's youngest generation has been scarred by genocide, and many are still impeded by an acute lack of resources needed for their basic survival, the children are ready to contribute to the healing. They need to have their voices heard as Rwanda moves toward national reconciliation. It was clear to the participants and others present that children's rights need to be placed at the top of the nation's agenda for any sustainable development. The

frank exchanges that occurred between the decision makers and the children in the legislative chambers led to a consensus that a forum is needed for the children so they can learn how to engage in constructive dialogue at the earliest stages of their careers.

The conference symbolized the emerging hope in Rwanda that out of the ashes of a genocide will grow a society based on the premise that respect for fundamental human rights is not a luxury reserved for a few of the world's inhabitants but a necessity for all of us, lest the evils of yesteryear visit us again.

In spite of and perhaps because of its past, Rwanda is striving to become a beacon of hope in the region. It is striving to build a society based on justice, respect, and tolerance for all and by all. It categorically rejects any form of discrimination or intolerance and affirms the need for humanity to celebrate diversity instead of using it as a basis for hatred and division.

The children of Rwanda are living an experience unique in the history of mankind. They are living in a society in which the victims of genocide must live side by side with their aggressors of yesterday, a society in which they have seen their friends, neighbors, and godfathers turn into implacable killers. Some of them have survived brutality from their own kith and kin, for the artificial barriers of Hutu, Twa, and Tutsi often broke down at the peak of the horror.

The world looked on in impotent horror as carnage was wreaked on their young minds and bodies. It should not look on as they struggle through the long process of healing and social reintegration that is just beginning. The thousands of child heads of households should not be left to carry the burden alone.

Rwanda's children are struggling to tell their story, a story to which humanity needs to lend an ear for its own survival. We must help them in the telling, we must listen to what they have to say, we must contribute to the healing. That is the very least we can do.

 cr rm pr m cr m pr m (illegible handwriting)

mkundaamahoromuruwandahose

"I love peace all over Rwanda."

Nubuntu abantu bonjyeye
Kubana babishima muma
horo ntamuriyane
Mumuco wa binyarwa

Namone P nti shiminabo
ndi kumwe na mama
Na barumuna banjye

*"I am glad that people have once again begun
to live together with no conflict.
I am also glad that I am still together with
my mother and my sisters."*

45

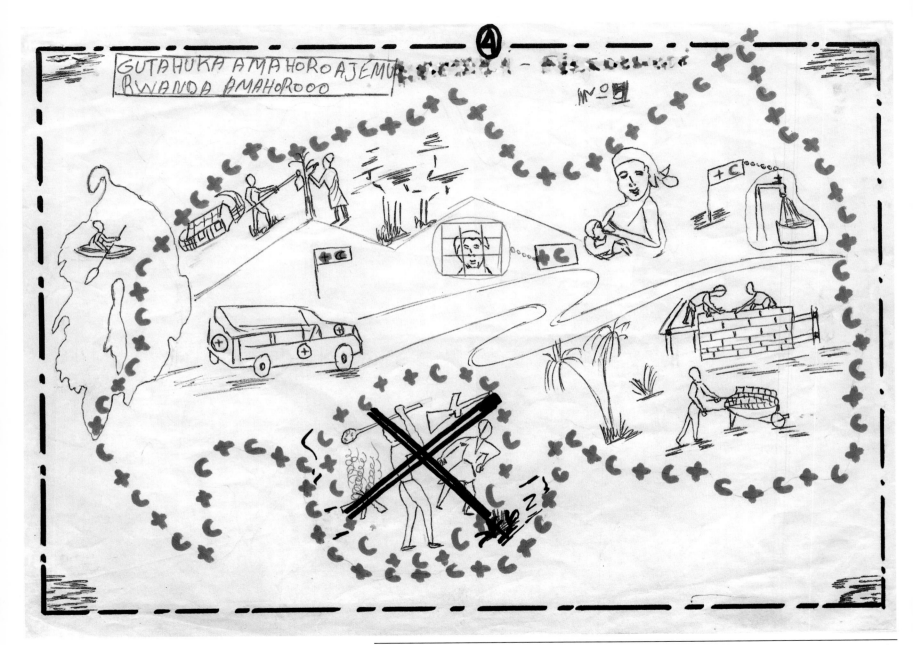

"Returning to a peaceful Rwanda"

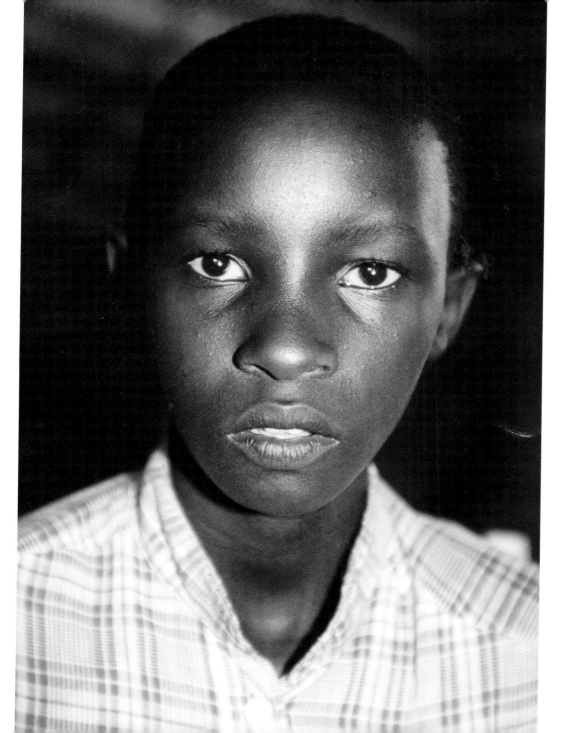

COLETTE, 14

Colette lives with her aunt. She remembers her younger brother being taken from her mother's arms before her parents were killed. "I was hiding in a tree and re-member thinking that if they found me they would kill me." When asked what she would like to do when she grows up, Colette replied, "If I fail, they will take me out of school." When pressed, she said, "I would like to be a teacher or a nun."

"Rwanda's children need help from sympathetic adults who can provide the children with...opportunities...to externalize their memories and put the pain and anxi-ety to rest. Only in this way can they become part of a better future as the twenty-first century dawns."

— AMBASSADOR RICHARD SEZIBERA

A schoolyard near Kigali, March 1999

"A truly inspirational book, *Witness to Genocide* not only presents the tragic tale of death and mutilation through the artwork of these young witnesses, but also tells of the hopes, dreams and wisdom of these children as they look to their future. This book is disturbing. It is also a sign of hope."

—AMBASSADOR ANDREW YOUNG, PRESIDENT, NATIONAL COUNCIL OF CHURCHES

A ROYALTY FROM THE SALE OF EACH BOOK AND ALL ADDITIONAL CONTRIBUTIONS WILL BE USED FOR THE TREATMENT OF TRAUMA IN RWANDA.

FRIENDSHIP PRESS
NATIONAL COUNCIL
OF CHURCHES

NEW YORK